EXPLORING THE WORLD OF REPTILES AND AMPHIBIANS

VOLUME 6

Spo–Xen

CHELSEA HOUSE
PUBLISHERS
An imprint of Infobase Publishing

Chelsea House

An imprint of Infobase Publishing
132 West 31st Street
New York, NY 10001

Library of Congress Cataloging-in-Publication Data

Green, Jen.
  Exploring the world of reptiles and amphibians / authors, Jen Green, Richard Spilsbury, Barbara Taylor.
       p. cm.
  Includes index.
  ISBN 978-1-60413-256-4
  1. Reptiles—Encyclopedias, Juvenile. 2. Amphibians—Encyclopedias, Juvenile. I. Green, Jen. II. Spilsbury, Richard, 1963- III. Taylor, Barbara, 1954- IV. Title.

  QL644.2.G737 2009
  597.9—dc22

For The Brown Reference Group plc
Project Editor: Sarah Eason
Designer: Paul Myerscough
Picture Researcher: Maria Joannou
Indexer: Angela Anstey-Holroyd
Cartographer: Darren Awuah
Design Manager: David Poole
Managing Editor: Miranda Smith
Editorial Director: Lindsey Lowe

Consultant Editor
John P. Friel, Ph.D.
Curator of Fishes, Amphibians and Reptiles
Cornell University Museum of Vertebrates
Ithaca, New York

Authors
Jen Green; Richard Spilsbury; Barbara Taylor

Picture Credits
Corbis: Frank Lane Picture Agency/Chris Mattison 20, 60, David A. Northcott 62; *Creatas*: 27, 30; *Dreamstime*: Roger Degen 18, Marianne Lachance 46, 47; *FLPA*: Foto Natura 8, Minden Pictures/Piotr Naskrecki 58; *Istockphoto*: Nancy Nehring 55, 56, Phillip Stollery 34, 35, Alan Tobey 39; *Photolibrary*: Oxford Scientific Films/Olivier Grunewald 10; *Photos.com* 40; *Photoshot/NHPA*: Jordi Bas Casas 48, Andrea Bonetti 49, James Carmichael Jr 53, T. Kitchin & V. Hurst 65, Bill Love 14, Otto Pfiste 57; *Science Photo Library*: Bob Gibbons 16; *Shutterstock*: Lynsey Allan 12, Bruce Amos 52, John Bell 13, 22, 23, Ryan M. Bolton 50, Joy Brown 24, 25, EcoPrint 4, Efiplus 45, David Hamman 54, Innocent 38, Joern 2, 19, Bruce MacQueen 51, William Attard McCarthy 42, Steve McWilliam 44, Stephen Meese 28, Snowleopard1 1, 31, 33, Judy Worley 43.

Artworks and maps © The Brown Reference Group plc

CONTENTS

INTRODUCING REPTILES AND AMPHIBIANS

Reptiles are some of the most feared animals on this planet. But only a few species are so deadly that they could kill someone. Most would rather run or slither away. What unites them all is that they are all cold-blooded creatures with scaly skin, which they shed to grow and replace worn-out skin. Reptiles cannot regulate their own body temperature, so they bask in the sunlight to warm up. Most reptiles lay eggs on the land, but a few species keep the eggs inside their bodies and then give birth to live young. With the exception of the crocodilians, most reptiles do not care for their young.

Like the reptiles, amphibians are cold-blooded animals. They are the link between animals that live in water and those that live on land. The majority of amphibians start their lives as eggs in the water. The eggs hatch as tiny larvae, which breathe in the water using gills. Through an amazing transformation called metamorphosis, these aquatic larvae become land-dwelling adults that breathe air through their lungs. Most amphibians also have the ability to breathe through their smooth, moist skin.

When you read books or surf the Internet to find information about reptiles and amphibians you might come across the word herpetology. Scientists often use this word to describe the study of reptiles and amphibians. Herpetology comes from the Greek word herpeton, meaning "creeping animal."

Exploring the World of Reptiles and Amphibians

From adders to xenosaurs, these six volumes of Exploring Reptiles and Amphibians contain more than one hundred articles that look at the amazing world of reptiles and amphibians. Some of the articles focus on a single species, such as the Indian cobra or Komodo dragon. Others talk about larger groups of reptiles or amphibians, such as lizards, snakes, or turtles. These overview articles are highlighted in bold typeface within the table of contents for each volume.

Each volume has a number of useful features, such as a family tree, which shows how reptiles and amphibians fit into the animal kingdom, how they are related to one another, and provides cross references to articles in this set; a glossary of terms used throughout the set; a further resources page, which includes information about good books to read or Web sites to visit; and a volume-specific index. Volume 6 contains a complete set index.

Within each article you will find a Fact File box, which summarizes the main features of the reptile or amphibian. It provides information about the breeding habits, coloration, diet, size, and status of a reptile or amphibian. Other items include Did You Know? boxes, which highlight some amazing facts about specific reptiles and amphibians, and box features that take a closer look at one interesting aspect of the creature in question. Throughout the book, large, colorful photographs and illustrations increase the reader's enjoyment and understanding of the world of reptiles and amphibians.

Family ties

Above each Fact File in every article there is a color bar that highlights in which particular group the reptile or amphibian belongs. There are four main groups of reptiles: crocodilians; snakes and lizards; turtles, terrapins, and tortoises; and tuataras. So there are four color codes for the reptiles. Amphibians are divided into three main groups: frogs and toads; newts and salamanders; and the wormlike caecilians. So there are three color codes for the amphibians. Just look at the color code to figure out in which group the animal belongs.

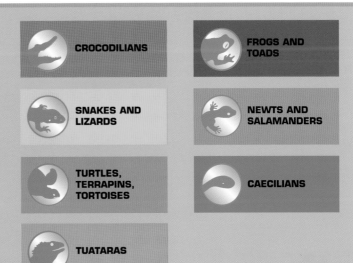

CROCODILIANS

FROGS AND TOADS

SNAKES AND LIZARDS

NEWTS AND SALAMANDERS

TURTLES, TERRAPINS, TORTOISES

CAECILIANS

TUATARAS

World Conservation Union (IUCN)

The World Conservation Union (IUCN) is the largest and most important conservation organization in the world. It aims to protect the natural world by promoting the conservation of animals and plants that are threatened with extinction. A living creature may be placed in one of the following categories in the *IUCN Red List of Threatened Species*:

- **Extinct**—there is no reasonable doubt that the last member of the species has died
- **Extinct in the wild**—the species survives only in captivity, in cultivation, or as a population well outside its past range
- **Critically endangered**—facing an extremely high risk of extinction in the wild
- **Endangered**—facing a very high risk of extinction in the wild
- **Vulnerable**—facing a high risk of extinction in the wild
- **Near threatened**—likely to qualify for a threatened category in the near future
- **Least concern**—is not threatened
- **Data deficient**—there is not enough information available to make an assessment

The IUCN status for the reptiles and amphibians in this book is highlighted at the foot of the Fact File panel in every entry.

Classifying reptiles and amphibians

Scientists like to group reptiles and amphibians into categories in which all the animals share certain body features. This is called classification. Animals that share body features are likely to be closely related because they have similar genes, which are the instructions found inside cells that tell the animal what to do. The family tree overleaf shows the relationships between all the different reptiles and amphibians. All the reptiles belong to the class Reptilia, while all the different amphibians belong to the class Amphibia. Scientists divided each class into several large groups, called orders, which contain more closely related reptiles or amphibians. In turn, each order comprises smaller groups called families. Families contain genus groups, which are collections of species—the smallest family unit. Reptiles or amphibians belonging to the same species can breed to produce offspring.

REPTILE AND AMPHIBIAN FAMILY TREE

ANIMAL KINGDOM (Animalia) → **Animals with a backbone** (PHYLUM Chordata, SUBPHYLUM Vertebrata) → **CLASS:**
BIRDS (Aves)
REPTILES (Sauropsida)
AMPHIBIANS (Amphibia)
FISH (Osteichthyes—bony fish, Chondrichthyes—cartilaginous fish)
MAMMALS (Mammalia)

The numbers below refer to volume and page numbers where a particular animal or group of animals is discussed in an article.

REPTILES

CROCODILIA (Alligators 1:18; Crocodiles 2:26)
- ALLIGATORS (American alligator 1:20; Caimans 1:62)
- CROCODILES (Gharial 3:8; Saltwater crocodile 5:38)

TUATARAS (6:34)

SQUAMATA
- **SAURIA** (Lizards 4:10)
- **SERPENTES** (Snakes 5:68)
- **WORM LIZARDS** (6:58)

TESTUDINES (Turtles 6:36, terrapins, tortoises 6:26)
- CHELYDRIDAE (Alligator snapping turtle 1:14)
- CHELIDAE (Matamata 4:28)
- CHELONIIDAE (Green turtle 3:42; Loggerhead turtle 4:16)
- DERMOCHELYIDAE (Leatherback turtle 3:72)
- EMYDIDAE (Eastern box turtle 2:36; Painted turtle 4:60)
- PELOMEDUSIDAE (Great South American river turtle 3:32; Spotted turtle 6:8)
- TESTUDINIDAE (Galápagos giant tortoise 2:62; Leopard tortoise 4:8)

AMPHIBIANS

CAECILIANS (1:56)

ANURA (Frogs and toads 2:56)

CAUDATA (Newts 4:52 and salamanders 5:32)
- AMBYSTOMIDAE (Axolotl 1:40; Tiger salamander 6:20)
- CONGO EELS 2:18
- GIANT SALAMANDERS 3:16 (Hellbender 3:46)
- NEWTS 4:52
- SALAMANDRIDAE (Eastern newt 2:38; Fire salamander 2:46; Rough-skinned newt 5:30; Sharp-ribbed newt 5:50; Smooth newt 5:64)
- PLETHODONTIDAE (Red salamander 5:26; Slimy salamander 5:60)
- PROTEIDAE (Mudpuppy 4:46; Olm 4:58)

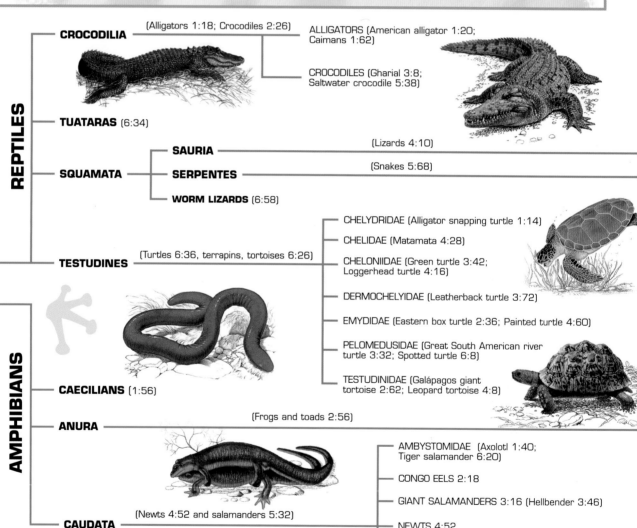

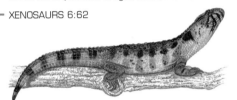

SPOTTED TURTLE

The yellow-spotted river turtle is named for the bright yellow spots on the sides of its head. These South American turtles are becoming rare because people have hunted them for their meat and eggs.

The yellow-spotted turtle is one of the largest river turtles in South America. Its oval-shaped shell can measure more than 2 feet in length. Apart from the spots on the head, which are brightest in younger individuals, yellow-spotted turtles have dull colors that blend in with their environment.

Yellow-spotted turtles live in lakes and slow-moving rivers in northern South America. During the rainy season, when the rivers overflow their banks, the turtles swim into the flooded forest rather than staying in the fast-flowing rivers. They spend most of their time in the water but sometimes come ashore to sunbathe in groups on sandbanks.

Breeding and Enemies

Yellow-spotted turtles breed in the dry season. Males and females mate in the water. Later, the female comes ashore at night to lay a clutch of fifteen to forty eggs high on a sandbank, shifting the sand to cover them with her hind feet. The young hatch about two months later.

Yellow-spotted turtles and their eggs are at risk from many predators. Tegu lizards and birds such as crested caracaras raid their nests for eggs. People also take the eggs and hunt the adult turtles for their meat. Spotted turtles are now rare, and in many countries it is illegal to hunt them. They are still targeted by poachers, however, because the larger Arrau River turtle—once the favorite prey of poachers—is now almost extinct.

Yellow-spotted turtles feed on water plants such as water hyacinths, and also like fruits that fall into the water. They will also eat snails.

Fact File

SPOTTED TURTLE

Podocnemis unifilis

Family: Pelomedusidae

Order: Testudines

Where do they live?: The Amazon River Basin in South America

Habitat: Lakes and slow-moving rivers and streams

Length: Shell up to 27 in. (69 cm) long

Weight: 20 lb. (9 kg)

Appearance: Dark brown or black shell is oval in shape; yellow or orange spots on the head fade as these turtles grow older

Diet: Water plants, fruits, and snails

Breeding: Females lay a clutch of 15–40 eggs, which hatch after 63 days

Status: Vulnerable

SURINAM TOAD

The Surinam toad is an odd-looking amphibian with a very flat, rounded body. The breeding habits of this toad are also rather unusual. The female carries her eggs on her back until they hatch into tiny toads.

Surinam toads live in dark, murky streams and swamps in northern South America and on the Caribbean island of Trinidad. They spend their lives in water, where their webbed hind feet make them very strong swimmers. They hunt fish, tadpoles, and other water creatures. The toad uses long, sensitive fingers on its front feet to feel for prey among the debris on the bottom. It can also detect tiny ripples caused by swimming creatures. The toad opens its large mouth to gulp in water and the prey, and uses its long fingers to push the meal into its mouth.

Breeding Behavior

Surinam toads are famous for their unusual breeding habits. The males call from below the water, producing a loud buzzing sound. A female that is ready to breed develops a pad of spongy material on her back. The male clasps her back legs from behind and above. The pair then turn somersaults in the water. At the top of every loop, the female lays one to three eggs, which the male then fertilizes and positions on her back. They repeat this process until up to 100 eggs are laid.

Over the next day, the eggs sink into the spongy flesh on the female's back until they are almost invisible. Each egg develops in a separate pocket of her flesh. The tadpoles develop inside the eggs and are carried around by the mother until fully developed. Three to five months later, the young toads hatch out.

The Surinam toad is very flat, with a small, flat head and upward-pointing eyes. The large, powerful hind legs have huge, flipperlike webbed feet.

Fact File

SURINAM TOAD

Pipa pipa

Family: Pipidae

Order: Anura

Where do they live?: Northern South America and Trinidad

Equator

Habitat: Backwaters, lakes, and dark, murky streams

Length: 5–8 in. (13–20 cm)

Appearance: Flat body with small, triangular head; large hind limbs have webbed feet; thin front limbs have long fingers; dark-gray mottled upper body, with pale underside

Diet: Tadpoles, fish, and other small aquatic creatures

Breeding: The female carries between 80 and 100 eggs on her back; eggs hatch after 11–19 weeks

Status: Common—least concern

TEGU

Tegus are among the world's largest lizards.
They live in the tropical forests of South
America, where they tackle prey as large
as snakes and small mammals.

Tegus are strong, sturdy lizards with cylindrical bodies, stout limbs, and thick tails. Their bodies are covered with small, shiny scales. There are at least six species. The common, or black-and-white, tegu is the most common species. It is found over a huge area of northern South America.

Predators and Prey

Tegus eat a variety of prey, from large insects to small mammals. They also raid farms in local villages to steal chickens' eggs. They bask in sunlight to warm up and usually hunt in the late afternoon. Tegus themselves are hunted by birds of prey, cats, and snakes. The young are more at risk from predators than the full-sized adults. People also kill tegus for their meat and skin and also because they steal eggs.

Forest Breeders

Tegu matings are timed so their eggs hatch in the rainy season when there is plenty of food. Courtship is quite dramatic. The male approaches the female with a stiff-legged walk, puffing himself up and snorting. He grabs the female and pins her down for mating. Females lay up to thirty eggs in a burrow, under leaves, or most often in a termite mound, which they tear open with their claws. The termites soon repair the mound, and seal in the eggs. The young tegus hatch and break out of the mound about three months later.

Tegus are widespread in the rain forests of South America. They dig burrows for themselves or take over the burrows of other animals.

Fact File

COMMON TEGU

Tupinambis teguixin

Family: Teiidae

Order: Squamata

Where do they live?: South America

Habitat: Clearings in rain forests and near villages

Length: Up to 43 in. (109 cm) from head to tail

Appearance: Large, powerful lizard with long head and thick tail; body is covered with small, shiny scales; adults are black, white, and yellow; young are bright green

Diet: Birds and their eggs, insects, lizards, small mammals, and snakes

Breeding: Females lay 7–30 eggs, which hatch after 12 weeks

Status: Common in suitable habitat

TERCIOPELO

The terciopelo is a member of the viper family. It is one of the most dangerous snakes in Central and South America. Every year, many people die from the bites of these poisonous snakes.

There are several reasons why terciopelos are so dangerous. First, these snakes commonly live alongside people. They are attracted to towns and villages because they contain abundant rats and mice, on which the terciopelos feed. In the wild, terciopelos live in forests, but their numbers actually increase when the land is cleared for farming. They have long fangs and strike rapidly. Most important, they are highly venomous. Their venom is quick-acting. It attacks the blood cells of their prey, causing death through severe internal bleeding.

Terciopelos also have superb camouflage, making them very difficult to spot. With brown or tan colors and pale triangular markings, they blend in perfectly with the leaf litter. This means it is all too easy to step on one without seeing it. Terciopelos are aggressive snakes and do not hesitate to defend themselves. They can strike from a coiled position over long distances. Even a snake that appears to be retreating may suddenly turn on an enemy and strike quickly, injecting large amounts of venom.

Together with its relative, the common lancehead, the terciopelo kills hundreds of people every year. In recent years, the number of deaths has dropped as medical care has improved in Central and South America, and also as more people have taken to wearing thick footwear. Even so, in a small country such as Costa Rica, terciopelos still kill about thirty people a year.

A terciopelo coils up into a defensive position ready to strike out and attack. These snakes are responsible for hundreds of lethal snakebites every year.

Fact File

TERCIOPELO

Bothrops asper

Family: Viperidae

Order: Squamata

Where do they live?: Central America to northern South America

Habitat: Fields, forest clearings, plantations, riverbanks, and villages

Length: 4–8 ft. (1.2–2.5 m)

Appearance: Large, stocky snake with triangular head; brown or tan with pale triangular markings

Diet: Invertebrates, birds, lizards, and small mammals, especially rodents

Breeding: Females give birth to a litter of 18–40 young 6 or 7 months after mating

Status: Very common

Distribution and Habitats

The terciopelo is a large, stocky snake that grows to 8 feet long. With its triangular-shaped head, it closely resembles its pit viper relative, the common lancehead. People used to think the two snakes were the same species, but they are found in different areas.

DID YOU KNOW?

- The terciopelo gets its name from the texture of its scales. *Terciopelo* is Spanish for "velvet."

- The terciopelo's relative—the common lancehead—is also called the fer-de-lance. It is named for the pointed shape of its head. *Fer-de-lance* is French for "lancehead." The common lancehead is also called the yellow-beard because of its pale-colored throat. Another snake called the fer-de-lance lives on the Caribbean island of Martinique.

GROUND DWELLER

In the wild, terciopelos mainly live in lowland forests. In some places, however, such as on the island of Trinidad, they live in the hills. In dry places, they live near water, which brings them into contact with people. They do well on sugarcane and banana plantations where rodents are plentiful. Terciopelos are nocturnal (come out at night). Adults live on the ground, where they hunt rodents. Heat-sensitive pits on their heads allow them to detect prey in the dark.

The terciopelo lives in Central and South America, from the eastern coast of Mexico south to Venezuela and northern Ecuador. The common lancehead is found farther east and south. Both species inhabit certain Caribbean islands.

Breeding

Terciopelos do not reproduce by laying eggs. Like most other vipers, they give birth to live young about six months after mating. The young snakes eat a wider range of prey than the adults, including insects, frogs, and lizards. The tip of the young snake's tail is pale yellow in color. By moving the tail over the ground, the tip of the tail looks like a crawling insect. This lures prey such as lizards, which are injected with a fatal dose of venom. Young terciopelos often climb into shrubs to hunt prey such as birds. The tail tip darkens as the young snake becomes older. Terciopelos are able to breed when they reach about 3 feet long.

The Breeding Season

Terciopelos breed at a particular time of year. However, the breeding season varies on either side of the Andes Mountains that run down Central

The female terciopelo is much longer and heavier than the male, with a bigger head, thicker body, and longer fangs.

and South America. Snakes that live east of the Andes Mountains mate in March and give birth in September or November. Snakes that live on the Pacific side of the Andes mate in September or November and give birth the following year, from April to June. In each case, mating is timed so that the young are born in the rainy season, when food is much more plentiful. Females that live along the Atlantic coast produce larger numbers of offspring than their Pacific-coast cousins. On average, the Atlantic-coast females produce more than forty young. Pacific-coast females bear only eighteen young.

17

THORNY DEVIL

Thorny devils are desert-dwelling lizards of Australia. The thornlike spines of these creatures are a form of defense against predators and also channel moisture into the mouth. These lizards feed exclusively on ants.

The deserts of western and central Australia are home to a lizard called the thorny devil. The spines of this unusual lizard deter attackers, but they also have another purpose. Water is almost impossible to find in the dry, sandy areas in which this lizard lives. Grooves between the spines channel the dew, which condenses on the lizard's body into its mouth. This supplies almost all of its needs for drinking water.

Life in the Burrow

Thorny devils live on the ground in underground burrows. They venture out by day to hunt ants. They can lick up twenty-five to forty-five ants per minute and eat 2,500 in a single sitting. Thorny devils move very slowly. They rely on their reddish-brown color to conceal them from predators. They can withstand great heat and are active when most other reptiles are hiding in the shade. Even so, they remain below ground during the hottest months of the southern summer (January and February). They also do not move around much during the coldest months (June and July).

For much of the year, thorny devils stay close to their burrows. These lizards are most active in spring and early summer. At this time they roam more widely, probably in search of mates. Little is known about the breeding behavior of thorny devils. However, females are known to lay a single clutch of between three and ten eggs in a deep, cool, south-facing burrow.

The thorny devil has thornlike spines all over its body, with larger spikes on its head and back and smaller ones on its legs.

Fact File

THORNY DEVIL

Moloch horridus

Family: Agamidae

Order: Squamata

Where do they live?: Western and central Australia

Habitat: Deserts

Length: 6–7 in. (15–18 cm)

Appearance: Stocky lizard covered with large, thornlike spines. Color varies from dark red to brown, with paler, wavy-edged stripes

Diet: Ants

Breeding: Females lay 3–10 eggs in burrows, which hatch after 90–132 days

Status: Common in suitable habitat

TIGER SALAMANDER

These large, colorful salamanders are some of
North America's best-known amphibians.
There are several varieties with different
colors and markings.

T iger salamanders are found over much of central and southern North America. They live in many different habitats, including deserts, forests, meadows, and scrublands, from sea level up to 11,000 feet. In cold places they hibernate in winter. Tiger salamanders live on the ground near water, usually hidden among plant debris. They are nocturnal, emerging at night to hunt earthworms, insects, small amphibians, and mice. In dry weather, they may travel to pools that are drying up to prey on tadpoles and insect larvae.

Life Cycle

The breeding habits of the tiger salamander depends on where they live. Most breed in early spring soon after they emerge from hibernation. They mate in water, usually after rain. The female lays a mass of about fifty eggs that stick to underwater plants. Some females produce more than 5,000 eggs in a single season. The larvae grow up in the water, hunting small aquatic creatures. Some large larvae feed on tadpoles and even on larvae of their own kind.

In warm, lowland pools the larvae usually change into adults in two to three months. In deserts, they mature before their pool dries up, usually in five to six weeks. In mountains, the larvae often pass the winter and become adults in the spring. Some larvae never mature into land-living adults but remain in pools. They can breed but keep the appearance of larvae.

Tiger salamanders have stout, cylindrical bodies with large heads and thick tails. There are at least six subspecies, which vary in color.

Fact File

TIGER SALAMANDER

Ambystoma tigrinum

Family: Ambystomatidae

Order: Caudata

Where do they live?: North America, including southern Canada and central Mexico

Habitat: Deserts, forests, meadows, mountains, and scrublands

Length: 7–14 in. (18–35 cm)

Appearance: Large, stocky animal with broad head, short limbs, and a thick tail. Color varies from black or gray to dark brown, with yellow or cream markings

Diet: Invertebrates, mice, tadpoles; some eat other salamanders

Breeding: Internal fertilization; females lay clumps of 50 eggs, which hatch after 20–50 days; larvae grow up in water

Status: Generally common, but some types are rare

TOKAY GECKO

This large, colorful lizard is named for its loud, barking "toe-kay" call. It lives in the forests of Southeast Asia but sometimes wanders into people's homes.

The tokay gecko is common throughout much of Southeast Asia. It lives in forests, where its large toe pads and ridged soles help it to climb trees. Tokay geckos are also common in towns and villages, where almost every building has its own gecko. People think that these lizards bring good luck. They certainly help to reduce pests, as they feed on insects and mice.

Tokay geckos are active at night. They spend the day hidden in cracks or under loose bark and emerge at night to feed. Creatures of habit, they emerge at the same time every night and move to a regular hunting position. They often lie in wait near spotlights to catch moths and other insects that are attracted to the light.

Tokay geckos are large lizards and have few enemies, but they may fall victim to some snakes. If attacked, they will put up a fight. They may even shed their tail to escape (the tail grows back again in three weeks.) They can deliver a painful bite and are hard to shake off once they have siezed something with their jaws.

Breeding

Male tokays have larger heads than the females. They are territorial and mate with several females who share their "patch." In most areas, tokays breed at any time of year. After mating, females lay two round, hard-shelled eggs under bark. Several females lay their eggs in the same place. The eggs hatch out in anything from sixty to two hundred days.

Experts think that the distinctive call of the tokay gecko helps neighboring reptiles to keep their distance so they do not compete for food.

Fact File

TOKAY GECKO

Gekko gecko

Family: Gekkonidae

Order: Squamata

Where do they live?:
Southeast Asia

Habitat: Forests, plantations, and buildings in towns and villages

Length: 8–14 in. (20–36 cm)

Appearance: Large, heavy-bodied gecko, with big head and large orange or yellow eyes; feet have wide toe pads; skin is bluish grey with pale or rust-colored spot; young are more boldly marked than the adults, with dark gray skin covered with large white spots and black-and-white striped tails

Diet: Insects, lizards, small birds, and rodents such as mice

Breeding: Females lay two (rarely three) hard-shelled eggs, which hatch after about 100 days

Status: Common

TOMATO FROG

The tomato frog lives on the island of Madagascar. The attractive markings and bright colors of this amphibian have made it popular among collectors, and it is now rare in the wild.

The tomato frog has an effective defense if its bright tomato color does not deter predators. When handled, the frog puffs itself up and releases a white slime from its skin. The slime may be poisonous or unpleasant-tasting to predators, and it gives people a skin rash. Tomato frogs belong to a family called the Microhylidae. About sixty species live on the island of Madagascar. They have varied habits, with some species living in trees and others in burrows.

Range and Habits

The natural habitat of the tomato frog is forest clearings in northeastern Madagascar. It also lives in the towns and villages that have developed there. Tomato frogs live on the ground and sleep in burrows. They are mostly active at night but may be seen around dawn and dusk, snapping up crickets and worms at the burrow entrance.

Breeding Behavior

Tomato frogs breed in pools, swamps, and water-filled ditches. After mating, females lay more than 1,000 eggs, which float on the surface. The tadpoles have flattened bodies. They filter food from the water using the mouth located at the very front of the head. Within about forty-five days they metamorphose (transform) into froglets. The young frogs lack the bright colors of the adults, being dull yellow with darker flanks.

Tomato frogs have large, prominent eyes. They are named for their tomato-red color, which acts as a warning signal to put off predators.

Fact File

TOMATO FROG

Dyscophus antongilii

Family: Microhylidae

Order: Anura

Where do they live?: Madagascar

Habitat: Forest clearings and wooded scrubland; gardens and plantations; larvae live in pools

Length: Males to 2.5 in. (6 cm); females to 4 in. (10 cm)

Appearance: Large red frog with narrow head and large eyes; skin smooth apart from a ridge running down each flank; flanks and hind limbs may have small, dark flecks

Breeding: Females lay more than 1,000 eggs in pools and ditches; tadpoles gradually change into the adult frogs over 45 days

Lifespan: Wild frogs live for 6–8 years; longer in captivity

Status: Near threatened

TORTOISES

Tortoises are land-dwelling reptiles. The main feature of these slow-moving creatures is their shells, which provide protection against predators. They are very easy to care for, so they are commonly kept as pets.

Tortoises and turtles make up the order (major group) called Chelonia, or shelled reptiles. Tortoises live exclusively on land, while turtles and terrapins spend part or all of their lives in fresh or salt water. There are around 240 different chelonians, but only thirty-eight species belong to the tortoise family.

Shape and Size

The most obvious feature of all the chelonians is their shells. The shell is made up of a bony inner layer and a horny outer layer. The horny layer consists of plates called scutes. The upper shell is called the carapace, and the lower shell is called the plastron. The shell is the tortoise's main defense against predators. When danger threatens, the tortoise withdraws its head and legs into its shell so that the whole body is protected. The disadvantage of the shell is that it makes the tortoise ungainly and slow-moving. Various tortoise species have shells of different shapes. Most shells have a fairly smooth surface, while a few are knobbly. In most species, the shell is domed, but the pancake tortoise has a flat shell.

The legs of the tortoise are strong and sturdy and support the weight of the shell. The head is small and sits at the end of a long, flexible neck. Most tortoises are brown, yellow, or olive-green, often with patterns on their scaly skin and shells. The colors and patterns camouflage the tortoise, helping it to blend in with its surroundings. Tortoises vary in size. The world's largest tortoise is the giant tortoise of the islands of Aldabra in the Indian Ocean. The carapace of these huge reptiles can measure up to 4.5 feet long and can

A leopard tortoise (top), Galápagos giant tortoise (middle), and two mating gopher tortoises (bottom).

weigh up to 550 pounds. At the other end of the scale, the speckled Cape tortoise is the world's smallest tortoise at just 2.5 inches in length.

Lifestyle

Tortoises live exclusively on land, but they often wallow in muddy pools to cool off in very hot weather. Most tortoises live in the warm, humid tropics. Those that live in the cooler temperate regions pass the cold winter months in a deep sleep called hibernation. Tortoises can be found in a variety of habitats, including forests and grasslands, but many live in deserts and dry scrubland. Desert tortoises can survive on very little water. Many species spend the hottest and driest months in a summer sleep, similar to hibernation, called estivation. Tortoises mainly eat plants, but some species also eat slow-moving creatures such as caterpillars, snails, and worms. They find their food using sight and smell.

▼ *The desert tortoise lives in burrows in order to escape the heat of the Mojave and Sonoran deserts, in the United States.*

Tough plant food is torn off and ground up in the tortoise's horny, beaklike mouth.

Tortoises reproduce by laying eggs. Some species produce several clutches in one year. During the mating season, the males fight for the right to mate with the females. The males charge and ram one another as each one tries to flip his rival onto his back. The defeated male will be helpless until he can right himself.

After mating, the females lay their hard-shelled or leathery eggs in a hollow in the ground, which they dig with their powerful feet. The females then refill the hole to hide the eggs from predators. The eggs hatch after two to fifteen months, and the hatchlings dig their way out.

Where Do Tortoises Live?

Tortoises are a widespread group of reptiles. Many species live in Africa, but they are also found in Asia, Europe, and the Americas.

Africa is home to the greatest number of tortoise species. The largest African species is the spurred tortoise, which measures up to 30 inches long. It lives on the edges of the Sahara Desert and survives drought by hiding in its

burrow. The tiny speckled Cape tortoise lives in rocky places in southern Africa. The island of Madagascar off the east coast of Africa holds four species that are now rare because of hunting and habitat loss. Species there include the attractive radiated tortoise, which has

DID YOU KNOW?

- The pancake tortoise of East Africa has a flat body, which allows it to retreat into rocky crevices and hide from predators. It wedges its shell behind a rock and becomes almost impossible to dislodge.

- The plowshare tortoise of Madagascar has a large prong on the front of its shell. The males use these prongs in the mating process.

LONG-LIVED REPTILES

Tortoises are some of the world's most long-lived animals. Scientists know about their long life from individuals kept as pets. Mediterranean spur-thighed tortoises are known to live for up to 160 years. In 1776, a giant tortoise from Aldabra was moved to a nearby island. It survived for 142 years but was fatally injured in an accident in 1918. The tortoise was a large adult when it was moved, so it must have been nearly 200 years old when it died.

starlike patterns on its shell. Spur-thighed tortoises are found in Africa and southern Europe. They are named for the distinctive spurs (horny spines) on their hind limbs. The biggest European tortoise is called the marginated tortoise and lives in Greece. This tortoise measures up to 1 foot in length.

Asian and American Tortoises

Seven species of tortoises live in Asia. They include the attractive star tortoise, with a shell pattern similar to the radiated tortoise. Elongated tortoises have an unusual, oval-shaped shell. The Burmese brown tortoise is the largest Asian species. The shell of this tortoise measures up to 18 inches in length.

New World tortoises include four species of gopher tortoises, which live in North America. Gopher tortoises make their homes in burrows. In South America, the Amazon River Basin is home to two forest species called the red-footed and yellow-footed tortoise. Both feed on a variety of plant material, including leaves and fruits. The yellow-footed tortoise is the larger of the two species, with a shell measuring up to 29 inches in length. The most southerly tortoise in the Americas is the Chaco tortoise of Chile and Argentina. This tortoise retreats to its burrow to hibernate (sleep) over the winter. The Galápagos Islands off the coast of Ecuador are home to ten subspecies of giant tortoises. Each one measures up to 4 feet long.

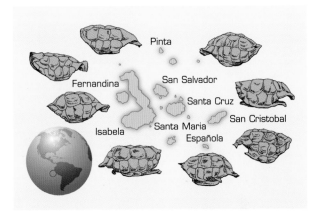

Pinta
San Salvador
Fernandina
Santa Cruz
San Cristobal
Santa Maria
Isabela
Española

🔺 *The "domed" and "saddleback" shells of the giant tortoises of the Galápagos Islands have evolved to suit the conditions on each island.*

The Most Northerly Tortoise

Horsfield's tortoise is found the farthest north of any tortoise, living on the plains of Kazakhstan in central Asia. This tortoise spends much of its life asleep. It survives the long, dry winter in hibernation. In spring, it emerges to feed and breed, before retreating to its burrow again in July to survive the summer drought.

DID YOU KNOW?

🏃 Hinged tortoises of Africa live in forests, grasslands, and semideserts. The rear end of the shells of these tortoises are hinged. They flap down to provide extra protection against predators.

🏃 The Burmese brown tortoise is unusual because it provides some parental care. The female guards her nest for a few days after she has laid her eggs.

TREEFROGS

Treefrogs are a large family of frogs. As their name suggests, treefrogs live mostly in the treetops. Sticky pads on their toes help them to clamber among the branches.

With more than 830 species, the treefrog family (Hylidae) comprises about one-fifth of all the frog species. Treefrogs live on every continent apart from Antarctica. Many treefrogs are native to the Americas, while just one species is found in Africa. Most treefrogs live in tropical rain forests. Some prefer cooler, drier habitats, such as the Australian "outback."

Most of the tropical treefrogs are nocturnal, which means they emerge at night. This helps them retain moisture. They spend the day hunched up with their legs tucked beneath them—a position that minimizes water loss. Some Australian treefrogs live in very dry places. These so-called water-holding frogs survive periods of drought by burrowing underground and shedding their outer layers of skin to form a watertight cocoon around their bodies.

Treefrog Types

The treefrog family is divided into four subgroups. Each one is distinguished by physical features and different lifestyles. The largest group is the typical treefrogs from northwestern Africa, Asia, Europe, and the Americas. These frogs have horizontal pupils and live in trees. The group also includes cricket frogs and chorus frogs, which live by lakes and pools, and four species of Mexican burrowing frogs.

The second group in the treefrog family is called the casque-headed frogs of Central and South America.

The pine barrens treefrog lives in the swamps and bogs of the southern United States. These frogs are facing extinction due to the loss of their habitat.

Fact File

TREEFROGS

The treefrog family (Hylidae) has around 835 species divided into four subfamilies: Hemiphractinae (casque-headed frogs and marsupial frogs), Hylinae (chorus frogs, cricket frogs, and other treefrogs), Pelodryadinae (Australian treefrogs), and Phyllomedusinae (leaf frogs)

Order: Anura

Where do they live?: Every continent except Antarctica

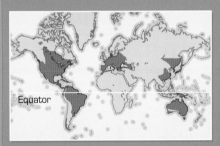

Equator

Habitat: Tropical forests; some live in temperate and dry regions

Length: 0.75–5.5 in. (2–14 cm)

Appearance: Small, slender frogs; color ranges from gray and green to brown; toes have rounded, sticky tips

Diet: Tadpoles eat plants; adults eat insects, spiders, slugs, and worms

Breeding: Females of most species lay their eggs in pools, streams, and ditches; some carry their eggs on their backs

Status: Mostly common; some species are rare

DID YOU KNOW?

🐾 Two species of American treefrog look so similar that scientists can only tell them apart by their different calls.

🐾 Gladiator frogs of Central and South America lay their eggs in basin-shaped nests at the edges of streams. The male stays nearby to guard the eggs and tadpoles.

They have bony skulls like helmets and eyes with horizontal pupils.

The third group is the Australian treefrogs. This group contains about 135 species that live in Australia and on islands of the South Pacific. They have horizontal pupils. Some live on the ground, including water-holding frogs of Australian deserts.

The fourth group is the leaf frogs from Central and South America. These frogs are large, tree-dwelling species with vertical pupils. The leaf frog group also includes the striking and distinctive red-eyed leaf frog, which is often featured in natural history television programs.

Breeding Time

Treefrogs that live in tropical rain forests usually breed at any time of year. Desert-dwelling frogs breed after the rainy season, while the frogs of the cooler temperate regions breed in the spring. The males form territories and call to attract the females. Each species has a slightly different call. When they mate, the male clasps the female just behind her armpits. Most species lay their eggs in quiet pools, slow-moving streams, and water-filled ditches. A few lay in fast-flowing water, and some use the tiny pools that form by water-filled tree-holes or cup-shaped plants called bromeliads.

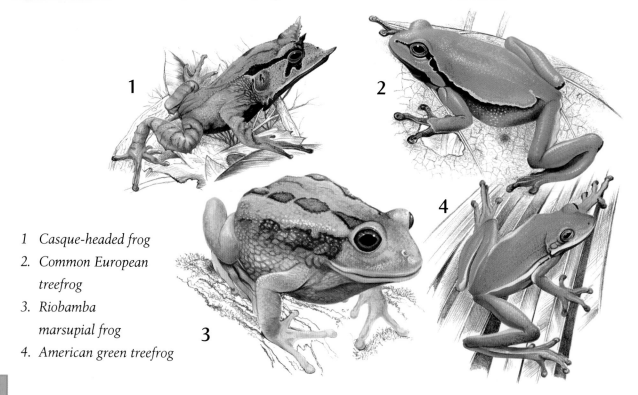

1   *Casque-headed frog*
2. *Common European treefrog*
3. *Riobamba marsupial frog*
4. *American green treefrog*

SIZE, SHAPE, AND COLOR

Treefrogs are well-suited to a life in the trees. The most obvious feature is the sticky pad at the end of each toe. Each pad acts like a suction cup to grip onto rough bark or smooth leaves. Treefrogs move slowly, but they leap to escape from their predators. Most are slender, with lightweight bodies suited to climbing. Larger species have huge toepads.

Most treefrogs are green or brown to blend in with the foliage. Some have bright marks that break up their outline and make it hard for predators to spot them. Some have bright spots on their thighs that appear as they leap and then disappear again, which confuses predators. Some treefrogs change color to match their surroundings or to give off signals.

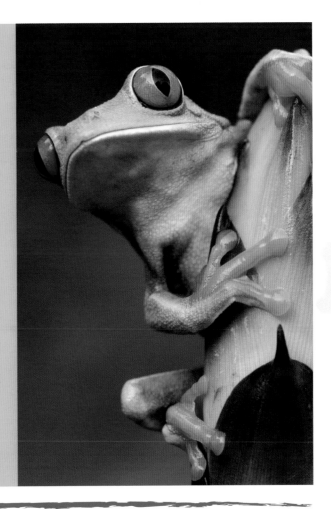

The tadpoles of most treefrogs grow up in water and feed on water plants. Leaf frogs lay their eggs on the leaves that overhang pools. Their tadpoles drop into the water when they hatch. Casque-headed treefrogs carry their eggs on their backs, sometimes in pouches. The young may be released as mature tadpoles or as tiny frogs.

Temperate Treefrogs

Treefrogs from temperate regions survive the cold winter months by hibernating. Their bodies contain a natural antifreeze that allows them to survive subzero temperatures. The spring peeper lives as far north as southeastern Canada. This frog is named for its peeping call, which announces the arrival of spring.

🔺 *The red-eyed leaf frog is one of the most familiar members of the treefrog family.*

33

TUATARA

Tuataras are the sole-surviving members of an ancient group of reptiles that thrived more than 200 million years ago. Today, tuataras live only on a few small islands off New Zealand.

Tuataras look like lizards, but they are the only survivors of a completely different group of reptiles called the beak-heads. The ancestors of tuataras lived on Earth around 220 million years ago. Fossils show they once thrived in Africa, Europe, and South America but had died out everywhere—except on New Zealand—by sixty million years ago. When people called Maoris landed on New Zealand around 1,000 years ago, they brought animals such as rats with them. Tuataras on the mainland died, but they survived on about thirty small offshore islands.

What Makes Them Different?

Unlike other reptiles, tuataras have two rows of teeth in their upper jaw, which mesh with a single row in the lower jaw. This helps them to grind up tough food. Tuatara hatchlings have a primitive third eye on top of their head that may be sensitive to light. Unlike most lizards, tuataras have no external openings to their ears.

Feeding and Breeding

Tuataras live in wooded areas of their island habitat. They stay in burrows by day and emerge at night to feed on invertebrates, lizards, and young birds. Tuataras breed in summer, and the males raise their crests to attract the females. After mating, the eggs start to develop inside the female, but are not laid until the following spring. Females lay eggs every two to five years.

> *"Tuatara" is a Maori word meaning "peaks on the back." The name refers to the spiny ridge that runs along the reptile's head, back, and tail.*

Fact File

TUATARA

Sphenodon punctatus

Family: Sphenodontidae

Order: Rhynchocephalia

Where do they live?: Small islands off New Zealand

Habitat: Coastal forests, usually near the burrows of seabirds

Length: 20–31 in. (50–80 cm)

Appearance: Large head, squat legs, long tail, and spiny crest on head and back; color ranges from green and gray to black with speckled markings

Diet: Insects, frogs, lizards, and the occasional birds' egg and chick

Breeding: Females lay 6–15 eggs, which hatch after 11–15 months

Status: Lower risk—least concern

TURTLES

Turtles are a major group (order) of reptiles that includes terrapins and tortoises. All the members of this group have a shell that provides protection against predators. Various species live in freshwater, saltwater, or on the land.

Reptiles with shells belong to the order Chelonia, or Testudines. Members of this group include the tortoises, turtles, and terrapins. In Britain, the word "turtle" is used only for species that live in the oceans. In North America, the word "turtle" refers to any species

1 Leatherback turtle
2. Hawksbill turtle
3. Loggerhead turtle
4. Green turtle

that lives in water. "Turtle" also refers to the entire group of shelled reptiles. In Britain, freshwater turtles are often called terrapins.

Body Basics

The most recognizable feature of these reptiles is their shell. It is is made up of an upper section, called the carapace, and a lower section, called the plastron. The outer layer is made up of horny, fused plates called scutes. The hard shell protects the turtle from predators and the weather. All turtles can draw their heads, limbs, and tails inside their shells.

Turtles pull their heads inside their shells in one of two ways. Members of the largest group of hidden-necked turtles pull their heads and necks back vertically to form a tight S-shape. This group includes tortoises. Side-necked turtles pull their head to one side. This group includes snake-necked turtles, some of which have a very long neck.

There are about 240 species of shelled reptiles, divided into twelve families. The largest family are the freshwater turtles, with eighty-six species. The thirty-eight species of land-living tortoises have sturdy legs to support their heavy weight. There are twenty-six species of softshell turtles with flexible, leathery shells. Marine turtles include six species of sea turtles and the leatherback turtle.

Lifestyle

Turtles vary in their feeding habits. Tortoises and many freshwater turtles (terrapins) usually

Fact File

TURTLES

Order: Testudines (Chelonia)

Where do they live?: Worldwide except the polar regions

Habitat: On land; freshwater and saltwater

Length: Carapace measures 2.5 in. (6 cm) to 6.5 ft. (2 m) long

Weight: 5 oz. (140 g) to 2,000 lb. (900 kg)

Appearance: Shelled reptiles with small heads, long necks, and powerful limbs; color ranges from yellow and olive-green to brown and black, with dark or pale markings

Diet: Varies according to species, including plants and invertebrates

Breeding: Females lay between 1 and 100 or more eggs in hollow dug in earth or sand; eggs hatch after 2–15 months

Status: Some species are common; some are rare

Lifespan: Some live for 100 years or more

eat plants. Most marine and some freshwater turtles eat other animals. Sea turtles prey on creatures such as jellyfish. Lacking teeth, all turtles use their sharp, beaklike jaws to slice through their food. Most turtles rely on their sense of smell to find food and also to locate mates. Scents are identified with the help of the Jacobson's organ in the roof of the mouth, which sends signals to the brain. Turtles can pick up scents underwater. They see well, and have color vision. Hearing is less important, which may explain why turtles make little noise. Many turtles have small, fleshy tentacles, called barbels, on their chin, which are used to find food. Barbels are touch-sensitive, allowing the turtle to probe for food as it swims along the bottom or in murky water.

All turtles reproduce by laying eggs on land. Marine turtles migrate long distances across entire oceans to reach the beaches where their species breeds. Clutch sizes vary according to species. Some lay a single egg, while others lay more than 100 eggs. After mating, the female digs a pit in the soft earth or sand with her hind limbs. She lays her eggs in the pit and then refills it. Eventually, the young turtles break out of their shells and dig their way to the surface.

▽ *The red-eared slider terrapin lives around the the Mississippi River south to the Gulf of Mexico.*

BODY PARTS

The skeleton of a turtle is quite unlike that of any other animal. Turtles have long, mobile necks to support their small heads. The short tail is also mobile, but the backbone and ribs are fused to the bottom of the carapace. This means the ribs do not help with breathing. Instead turtles have special leg muscles that help to draw air into the lungs and expel waste air. Lacking the gills of fish, aquatic turtles have to surface to breathe air. However, some turtles have special organs in their throat, which extract oxygen from water. Others have long nostrils that act as snorkels.

Land tortoises have stout, pillarlike legs. Aquatic species have webbed feet or limbs shaped like flippers (see right).

The legs are scaly and the feet are clawed. Tortoises have short claws that become blunt as they walk, while aquatic turtles have longer claws.

The First Turtles

The ancestors of modern turtles appeared on Earth about 280 million years ago. Very early species had flexible shells. By about 200 million years ago, turtles had developed hard shells. These early turtles lived in water and looked a lot like modern species, but they had teeth. Over time, the turtles lost their teeth and developed beaklike mouths. Around 90 million years ago, the largest chelonian ever known, called *Archelon*, roamed the seas. With a shell measuring at least 12 feet long, *Archelon* was a third longer than the largest living species, the leatherback turtle.

DID YOU KNOW?

- Snapping turtles lie in wait for their prey on the beds of shallow lakes and rivers. They snap up prey with their strong jaws.

- Leatherback turtles make the longest migration of any turtle, from their feeding grounds to the remote beaches on which they breed. They have been known to migrate over 12,000 miles.

VIPERS

Vipers make up a large family of snakes. The best-known are the rattlesnakes from the Americas. Every year, hundreds of people die from the bites of these venomous snakes.

Vipers such as this adder have raised scales that look like horns. They break up the outline of the snake's head, making it harder for predators to see.

All vipers are extremely poisonous. They use their venom to kill prey and defend themselves from attack. The long, hollow fangs that inject the venom are located on a hinged bone in the upper jaw. When not in use, the fangs fold back against the roof of the mouth and are covered by a fleshy sheath. As the snake strikes, the fangs swing forward to stab the prey and inject the lethal poison. Vipers are lithe, thick-bodied snakes with short, thin tails. Poison glands on either side of the jaw make

the head wide. Vipers vary in size from just 11 inches to more than 6 feet in length.

The Viper Family

Vipers are found nearly all over the planet. They survive in many different habitats and can be found farther north and south than any other snakes. The adder is the most northerly species, while the Patagonian lancehead is the most southerly. Vipers also live at higher altitudes than any other snakes—up to 16,000 feet in the case of the Himalayan pit viper. Various viper species live in Africa, Asia, Europe, and the Americas. Vipers are notably absent from Australia and the island of Madagascar.

The viper family contains about 250 species, making up about one-twelfth of all snakes. The family is divided into two main groups: "true" vipers and pit vipers. There are also six species of night adders and the Fea's viper, which is an unusual snake from the remote Himalayas. Night adders live in Africa and specialize in hunting toads. Like Fea's viper, they have smooth scales on their bodies and large scales on their heads.

Pit Vipers

Two-thirds of all vipers are pit vipers. Members of this group are found in Asia, eastern Europe, and the Americas. Pit vipers are named for the heat-sensing pits on their heads. These are used to detect the body heat of prey such as birds and mammals. The ability to detect heat allows the snake to hunt in total darkness. Many pit

vipers are night hunters. They live in various habitats, including deserts, forests, and swamps.

Pit vipers include the familiar rattlesnakes, which are named for the "rattle" of loose scales on their tails. Rattlesnakes shake their rattles to warn away intruders, such as cattle, that might tread on them. There are about thirty species of rattlesnakes, and they live in the Americas. Pit vipers feed mainly on warm-blooded prey.

They track down this prey using their heat-sensing pits. Rattlesnakes eat a wide range of prey, including insects, fish, frogs, young alligators, hares, and ground squirrels.

Coping with the Cold

Vipers that live in cold places spend the winter months in hibernation. They emerge in the spring and warm their bodies by basking in the sunlight. Their dark skin quickly absorbs heat.

▼ *The viper's heat-sensing pits are found on either side of the head, between the eye and the nostrils.*

TRUE VIPERS

About one-third of vipers are Old World adders or "true" vipers. They are found throughout Africa, Asia, and Europe. True vipers are short and stocky, with wide, triangular or pear-shaped heads. They have "keeled" or ridged scales. True vipers live in various habitats, including deserts, forests, mountains, and scrub. Many species are very well camouflaged. Species such as the Gaboon viper (see right) of Africa have brown, yellow, and black markings to conceal the snake in the forest leaf litter. Some tree-dwelling vipers are green to blend in with their surroundings.

Many adders have raised scales that look like horns on their heads, either over the eyes or on the snout. These ridges help to protect the eyes or nostrils from sand and dust and also break up the outline of the snake's head so that it is hard to spot. Saw-scaled and carpet vipers can produce a rasping sound by rubbing their keeled scales together. They do this to frighten away intruders. Old World adders and vipers eat a variety of different prey, including birds, lizards, and small mammals such as rodents. In most species, females carry the eggs inside their bodies, and the young hatch as live snakes. A few reproduce by laying eggs.

Vipers are usually well-camouflaged and can risk basking in the open. These snakes are also stocky, which helps to retain body heat. Female vipers that live in cold places carry their developing eggs inside them and give birth to live young. They can regulate the temperature of the young by basking. Some species also feed their young using their own blood.

VIVIPAROUS LIZARD

The viviparous lizard lives farther north than any other lizard. It can even be found within the Arctic Circle. It has unusual breeding habits, giving birth to live young instead of laying eggs.

The viviparous lizard belongs to a large family of lizards called the Lacertidae. This slender, long-tailed lizard lives throughout Europe and central Asia from Britain eastward to Japan. Within this vast area, viviparous lizards thrive in many different habitats, including bogs, coastal regions, ditches, meadows, moors, and mountains up to 8,200 feet.

Viviparous means "bearing live young," and this helps these lizards survive in cold, northerly climates. Viviparous lizards pass the cold winter months in hibernation. In the northernmost part of their range, they may spend up to eight months of the year asleep.

Feeding and Breeding

Viviparous lizards feed mainly on invertebrates. In turn, they are eaten by birds, larger lizards, small snakes, and mammals such as weasels. Their main form of defense is escape, and can shed their tail in an attempt to do so.

Viviparous lizards live in colonies centered on a good basking area. Mating takes place soon after the lizards emerge from hibernation. Unlike all other lacertids, female viviparous lizards give birth to live young. Up to eleven young develop inside the female. As the mother basks in the sun, she warms the young inside her. This helps them to develop quickly. In a few places, however, viviparous lizards lay eggs, which hatch in four to five weeks. Young are born inside a transparent membrane (skin) from which they emerge within minutes.

The color of the viviparous lizard varies according to the place in which it lives. Most are brown, but these lizards can also be gray, olive, and black.

Fact File

VIVIPAROUS LIZARD

Zootoca vivipara

Family: Lacertidae

Order: Squamata

Where do they live?: Most of Europe eastward across Asia to Japan

Habitat: Cliffs, ditches, dunes, hedges, marshes, and moors

Length: 6 in. (15 cm)

Appearance: Small lizard with short legs and long tail; color ranges from olive to gray, with white, yellow or orange belly; females have a single dark stripe running down the back; males are much darker

Diet: Insects and their larvae, and spiders

Breeding: Most females give birth to 3–11 live young after a gestation period of 8–13 weeks; some lay eggs

Lifespan: Up to 12 years

Status: Common in suitable habitat

WALL LIZARDS

Wall lizards get their common name for their habit of basking on walls in the sunshine. Also known as the lacertids, some species in this large family can be found in remote deserts, while others live alongside people in towns and villages.

The family of lizards called the Lacertidae are known by many common names, including the wall lizards, sand lizards, and Old World lizards. There are about 280 species in the group. They live in Africa, Europe, and right across Asia, from the Middle East to Japan. These reptiles are mostly medium-sized, slender lizards with long legs and a long tail. The scales on their backs are small and beadlike, while the scales that cover the head and underside are much larger. Many lacertids are well-camouflaged with dull browns and grays. Others are brightly colored, especially the males during the breeding season. Some species from the islands of the Mediterranean Sea are a brilliant shade of green or blue and are striking to look at.

Feeding Habits

Wall lizards feed mostly on invertebrates such as insects, slugs, and spiders. Some species vary their diet throughout the year as different insects become more and less available. For example, they may switch from beetles to ants or mayflies when these insects hatch in the summer. Some wall lizards eat plants as well as insects. Island species feed almost entirely on fruit, flowers, and pollen. Others are brave enough to steal scraps of food from predators. For example, some wall lizards live near seabird colonies and scavenge the scraps of fish dropped by the birds. The brave Lilford's wall lizard even steals the scraps from falcons' nests.

The common wall lizard is a small, slender reptile that lives throughout Europe and has also been introduced to North America.

Fact File

WALL LIZARDS

Family: Lacertidae, 279 species in 26 genera

Order: Squamata

Where do they live?: Africa, Europe, and Asia

Equator

Habitat: Varied, including forests, grasslands, mountains, deserts, towns, and villages

Length: 4–32 in. (10–80 cm)

Appearance: Slender, long-tailed lizards with small scales on the back and larger scales on the head and belly; many species are camouflaged in shades of brown, black, green, or yellow; other species are bright green or blue

Diet: Earthworms, insects, slugs, spiders, and other invertebrates; some species eat small lizards; others eat plants

Breeding: Females of most species lay 4–20 soft-shelled eggs, which hatch in 30–45 days. The viviparous lizard gives birth to live young; five species reproduce without mating

Status: Varies from common to scarce

Life Cycle

Most wall lizards breed in the spring, but some tropical species breed at any time of the year. Males become more brightly colored during the mating season. They also form a territory, in which each male defends a "patch" of land that contains several females. The male uses scent to mark the borders of his territory. Then he takes up an aggressive stance to warn away his rivals. He lifts his head and puffs his throat as an threatening display. These visual signals usually work, but if not a fight will break out. Tails are often broken as each male tries to bite the other. Finally, the loser is chased away.

◁ *The Ibiza wall lizard lives in the shrublands of rural Spain.*

Almost all wall lizards reproduce by laying eggs. Females lay clutches of between four and twenty soft-shelled eggs in short burrows. The eggs hatch within forty-five days. The viviparous lizard is an exception. In this species, the female carries the eggs inside her body and gives birth to living young. Indeed, the word *viviparous* means live-bearing. Females from a few species from the Caucasus region of Eurasia can produce offspring without mating. This highly unusual method of reproduction is called parthenogenesis. This practice was first discovered in lacertids. Several other lizard species are also known to reproduce in this way.

Escaping Danger

Many predators feed on wall lizards, including birds, larger lizards, and snakes. Wall lizards rely mostly on speed and agility to escape from predators. If seized, they can shed their tail, which continues to wriggle as a distraction while the lizard escapes. The lizard does not lose its tail for good—it simply grows back again about three weeks later.

ADAPT TO THE HABITAT

Wall lizards are found in many parts of Africa, Asia, and Europe, from tropical rain forests and arid deserts, through temperate grasslands, to the cold tundra far north of the Arctic Circle in the case of the viviparous lizard. Many unique species live on islands, for example, in the Mediterranean and on the Canary islands west of Africa. Many wall lizards, such as the Balkan wall lizard below, can be seen basking on walls in towns and villages to warm up. Some species never stray far from people, while others prefer to hide in the dense vegetation of the rain forest or beneath the scorching desert sand. Desert-dwelling wall lizards include the sand-swimmers of the Namib Desert in southwestern Africa. Some desert species have fringed scales on their toes that allow them to run over sand. They dive into loose sand to escape predators and avoid the strong heat of the midday Sun. Forest-dwelling wall lizards have features that help them to climb trees. For example, the African blue-tailed tree lizard has rough scales under its tail that grip the tree bark. Several African keel-bellied lizards can grip twigs with their tail, which acts as a fifth limb. Asian grass lizards are also strong climbers, and can climb tall grass stems. They can wriggle their whole body to "swim" through the grass at speed.

WATER FROGS

Water frogs are one of the largest families of frogs and toads. Found in most parts of the world, the family includes familiar species including the common European frog and the North American bullfrog.

Water frogs belong to a large family called the Ranidae. They are also called "typical" frogs, true frogs, and ranids. Water frogs are some of the most important species because of their wide distribution and also because they are so common. Most water frogs have slim bodies with narrow heads, long, powerful hind legs, and webbed feet. Members of the family vary in size from the microfrog of southern Africa, which measures just 0.75 inch long, to the African Goliath frog, which grows to 1 foot or more. Most water frogs have narrow waists and smooth skin. Many have a pair of ridges running down the sides of their backs. Within this huge family, there are many species that differ from the general description. Some are plump or squat, rough-skinned, and toadlike, while others are unusually slender.

Distribution and Way of Life

Water frogs live almost everywhere frogs are found. They are particularly abundant in the Northern Hemisphere. One species, called the North American wood frog, lives inside the Arctic Circle. Water frogs are found on every continent except Antarctica. There are relatively few species in South and Central America and Australia, and there are none in New Zealand.

As their name suggests, the water frogs live beside freshwater, which they use as an escape route from predators and as a source of food for themselves.

The bullfrog is one of the largest species in the family of true frogs. These large frogs spend almost all of their lives in the water.

Fact File

WATER FROGS

Family: Ranidae is made up of 729 species divided into eight subfamilies: Raninae, Dicroglossinae, Platymantinae, Tomopterninae, Ptychadeninae, Petropedetinae, Pyxicephalinae, and Ranixalinae

Order: Anura

Where do they live?: The Americas, Africa, Australia, Europe, and Asia including Southeast Asia

Equator

Habitat: By water and in fields, meadows, woods, forests and gardens, also some in drier areas

Length: 0.75–12 in. (1.8–30 cm)

Appearance: Mostly slim, smooth-skinned frogs with pointed heads, long hind limbs, and webbed feet. Most are green or brown, with darker markings

Diet: Insects, spiders, and other invertebrates

Breeding: Most lay thousands of eggs in water that hatch into tadpoles and later transform into adults

Status: Varies from common to endangered

DID YOU KNOW?

- The semaphore frogs of Southeast Asia communicate by sticking their legs out to one side and spreading their toes to show the bright blue webbing between them. Semaphore frogs live by fast-flowing streams. They probably developed this visual signal because vocal calls could not be heard over the water.

- The sand frogs of southern Africa spend the dry months of the year in underground burrows. They emerge to breed in the temporary pools that form after heavy rain.

Water frogs live by lakes, ponds, rivers, and streams as well as gardens, fields, forests, lakes, meadows, ponds, and woodlands. A few species live by the semi-salty water of the coastal regions or by warm springs. Some species also live in burrows and look like burrowing toads, while others climb trees and have large, sticky toepads that help them grip.

Adult water frogs are predators and feed on insects, spiders, and other small creatures. These frogs gather at the start of the breeding season, with the males calling to attract the females. The male grips the female's body with his front legs to mate. He fertilizes the female's eggs as they are laid. The eggs are usually laid in the water in large clumps. Each egg is surrounded by jelly to protect it. Females can lay thousands of eggs, but most die or are eaten by predators. Only a small fraction of the eggs survive to become adults. Most young pass through the tadpole stage before becoming adults. In a few species, however, the eggs hatch directly into froglets.

▽ *An American bullfrog hides in the tall grass to escape predators.*

Water Frog Subfamilies

There are 730 species of water frogs in the family Ranidae. There are eight subfamilies. The largest family, the Raninae, has more than 250 species. They can be found across Africa, Australia, the Americas, and Eurasia. The group includes the most familiar species, including the American bullfrog and the common European frog. It also includes rare species such as the long-toed stream frogs of southern Africa, and the torrent frogs of China and Southeast Asia.

The subfamily Dicroglossinae includes more than eighty species that live in Africa, Asia, and the island of Fiji. The group includes the massive Goliath frog, the crowned bullfrog of Africa, and the Indian bullfrog, which has fierce, predatory tadpoles. The group also contains rice-paddy frogs that are common in paddies and villages throughout southern Asia. Another large subgroup, called the Petropedetinae, contains more than 100 species of frogs from southern Africa. The largest is just 2 inches long. The subfamily Platymantinae has many species that are unique to one island or group of islands, such as the Solomon Islands frogs (see the box right).

TRUE COLORS

Most water frogs are brown or green in color, with darker or paler markings that help to conceal their bodies among the stones, earth, or vegetation. The shape, markings, and color of the Solomon Islands leaf frog (shown below) look exactly like a dead leaf. This helps to camouflage the body of the frog against the leaf litter. Some common water frogs have a dark "mask" around their eyes, which stretches from the snout to the neck. A few species are more brightly colored. For example, the palm frog has a jade-green back, yellow feet, and large blue eyes. It lives among the trees of tropical and subtropical forests in Papua New Guinea and the Solomon Islands.

WHIPTAILS

Whiptails, racerunners, and jungle racers belong to a large family of lizards called the teiids. These alert, fast-moving lizards live in a wide range of habitats in the Americas.

Whiptails belong to a family of lizards called the Teiidae. There are two main groups in this family—the racerunners and the jungle racers. There are about sixty species of racerunners that live in the Americas. Around thirty-three species of jungle racers live in Central and South America. The family also includes the tegus—large lizards from South America. In total there are about 120 different kinds of teiids.

These medium to large reptiles have the typical lizard body shape, with a narrow, pointed head, long legs, and a long tail. They range in size from the little striped whiptail, which measures just 2 inches long excluding the tail, to the large tegus, which measure 2 feet long excluding the tail. Racerunners are usually striped in dull colors, but some tropical species have bright green or blue markings. Jungle racers are powerful lizards, and they can often be heard crashing through the undergrowth. Tegus are large lizards found in South America. The family also includes the caiman lizard and the crocodile tegu, which are semiaquatic species. Some scientists also place the group of spectacled lizards, with 179 species, within the Teiidae family.

Breeding Behavior

All teiids reproduce by laying eggs. In cold places, these reptiles breed as soon as they emerge from hibernation in the spring. Tropical species breed at any time of the year but mostly to coincide with the rainy season.

The long, slender body of the plateau striped whiptail has several white stripes down its back and sides. The underside is white or pale blue-green.

Fact File

WHIPTAILS AND OTHER TEIIDS

Family: Teiidae, 120 species in nine genera: *Cnemidophorus* (racerunners), *Ameiva* (jungle racers) *Callopistes* (false tegus), *Crocodilurus* (the crocodile tegu), *Dicrodon* (deserts tegus), *Dracaena* (caiman lizards), *Kentropyx* (whiptails), *Teius*, and *Tupinambis* (tegus)

SPECTACLED LIZARDS

Family: Gymnophthalmidae (179 species in 34 genera)

Order: Squamata

Where do they live?: The Americas, including some Caribbean islands

Equator

Habitat: Deserts, forests, farms, scrub, villages, and coastal regions

Length: 2 in. to 2 ft. (5–61 cm) long

Appearance: Medium to large lizards, dull brown or cream with stripes; some have green or blue markings

Diet: Small invertebrates

Breeding: Females lay 3–30 eggs; some reproduce without mating

Status: Varies from common to endangered

HABITAT AND LIFESTYLE

Whiptails, such as the four-striped whiptail shown below, are diurnal reptiles, which means they are active during the day. Early in the morning, these lizards bask in the Sun to raise their body temperature and hunt for food. Whiptails often live in forest clearings, including those around farms and villages. In such places, there are plenty of good basking

spots, as well as cover to conceal the lizard if danger threatens. Jungle racers live in forest clearings and grasslands in tropical regions. Tegus also live in the open forest, as well as along the banks of rivers and streams. Some racerunners inhabit deserts and scrubland, including in North America. Desert species hunt in the morning and at dusk and spend the hottest part of the day in cool, shady burrows. Other racerunners live by the coast on the islands of the Caribbean. In the far north and south of their range, whiptails hibernate in winter and may only be active for six months of the year.

Whiptails eat mainly insects and other small creatures. Tegus eat a range of prey including fruit, snails, fish, frogs, other lizards, and carrion (dead meat). The teiids have good eyesight, which helps them spot food from a distance. Like snakes, these lizards also have long, forked tongues to help them gather scents in the air. The lizard then "smells" the scent by touching the tongue on the Jacobson's organ in the roof of its mouth.

This is when food is most abundant. Females lay between three and thirty soft-shelled eggs. Some racerunners can produce young without mating in a process called parthenogenesis. All the lizards of such species are female, and they lay fertile eggs without mating. Parthenogenetic species include the desert grassland whiptail of Arizona. Females lay up to four eggs that hatch into young with bright blue tails.

DID YOU KNOW?

- The caiman lizard and the crocodile tegu live by the rivers and streams of the Amazon River Basin. The crocodile tegu has a flat tail like a crocodile, which it sweeps from side to side to move through the water. It eats frogs, fish, and other water creatures.

- Caiman lizards have two rows of scales running down their backs and tails.

Rainbow whiptails are brightly colored lizards that live in Colombia.

Spectacled Lizards

The spectacled lizards are named for their fused lower eyelids, which look a little like spectacles. There are around 179 species, some of which are called shade, creek, root, or cave lizards. Being small, spectacled lizards are sometimes called microteiids. These shy creatures dwell on the ground in the leaf litter or under rotting tree stumps. They can be very hard to spot. Many have short limbs. Some are legless and these can only move by wriggling like a worm. Spectacled lizards eat caterpillars, grubs, and worms. They breed by laying small clutches of eggs.

WORM LIZARDS

Worm lizards, or amphisbaenians, are slender, legless reptiles. Like earthworms, they spend their lives in underground burrows. Scientists know very little about these unusual creatures.

A mphisbaenians are commonly called worm lizards, but they are neither worms nor true lizards. Scientists think that their closest relatives are snakes and lizards. Experts in classification place the unusual worm lizards in the same order (Squamata). Snakes, lizards, and worm lizards are thought to be descended from common ancestors.

At first glance, amphisbaenians look exactly like earthworms, with their long, thin bodies and pink skin. Most worm lizards do not have any legs, but three species have tiny forelimbs. Worm lizards have blunt heads and short, round tails. The word *amphisbaenian* is a Greek word which means "to go both ways." The name may refer to the fact that it is often difficult to tell the tail ends from the heads of these creatures.

Living Underground

Like earthworms, amphisbaenians are well-suited to their underground lifestyle. They have square scales arranged in rings around the body. The tiny eyes are covered by scales and show up as dark spots. Worm lizards can tell light from dark, but their eyes cannot produce a visible image. They have no external ear openings, and their nostrils point backward so soil does not enter while burrowing. Most species are pink or white, but some have darker markings.

Worm lizards spend their entire lives in tunnels. Some species appear on the surface after heavy rain.

*The worm lizard Amphisbaena vanzolinii **is a legless amphibian. The eyes of this wormlike amphibian are dark spots that can tell light from dark.***

Fact File

WORM LIZARDS

The suborder Amphisbaenia consists of three families: Amphisbaenidae (155 species) Trogonophidae (short-headed worm lizards, six species) and Bipedidae (two-legged worm lizards, three species)

Order: Squamata

Where do they live?: The Americas, Africa, southern Europe, Middle East

Habitat: Varied, including rain forests, woodlands, grasslands, and deserts

Length: Up to 30 in. (75 cm) long

Appearance: Long, slender, wormlike white or pink reptiles; some species have dark markings; most lack limbs; eyes show up as dark spots

Diet: Insects and earthworms; large species also eat small vertebrates

Breeding: Most lay eggs, a few give birth to live young

Status: Mostly not known

Most are only seen above ground if rain floods their burrows. They move through their tunnels by sliding their loosely attached skin forward over their bodies, like pulling down the sleeve of a sweater. Then they brace their scales against the sides of the tunnel and pull the inner cylinder of their body forward. When they move quickly, this two-stage process produces a rippling effect.

Three Families

Amphisbaenians have only a limited ability to control the temperature of their bodies. For this reason, they are found only in warm regions. Various species live in rain forests, woodlands, grasslands, and dry places around the world, including deserts. There are 164 species of worm lizards. Experts divide the group into three families, of which the largest, the amphisbaenids, contains 95 percent of the group. Members of this large family are mostly found in tropical South America, southern Africa, and parts of North America, North Africa, southern Europe, and the Middle East. The Florida worm lizard is the only amphisbaenian found in the United States.

The second family is the short-headed worm lizards (also called the trogonophids). There are six species in this small family. The bodies of this small group of worm lizards are roughly triangular in cross-section. They specialize in digging through loose, sandy soil and are found in scattered parts of North and East Africa, the Arabian Peninsula, and on Socotra Island in the Indian Ocean.

The third family, the bipedids, contains just three species, which differ from all the other worm lizards in having small but strong front legs. These tiny forelimbs are found near the head and come with long claws to help burrow through the soil. These two-legged amphisbaenians are found only in western Mexico.

Unlike most species, the ajolote has two small forelimbs, which it uses to burrow through the soil.

Way of Life

Worm lizards move about their burrow networks to find food and their mates. Most worm lizards feed on invertebrates such as insect grubs and earthworms. Some large species also prey on small vertebrates, such as lizards. Amphisbaenians usually eat creatures that fall into their tunnels. They also lie in wait just below the surface to ambush small creatures walking on the surface. When they sense movement above, they break through the surface to snatch their prey and drag it underground. The tunnel networks often connect to an ant or termite nest, which provides a rich source of food in the form of grubs.

Scientists know little about the life cycle of amphisbaenians. Most lay eggs, with some species laying their eggs in ant or termite nests. When their young hatch out they feast on the insects. In some worm lizard species, the female carries the eggs inside her body and then gives birth to live young.

TUNNELLING TECHNIQUES

Worm lizards have hard, ridged skulls to tunnel through the soil. Many have pointed heads to force their way through (1). Others have wedge-shaped heads and bony plates with hard cutting edges to scrape at the soil (2). They squash the soil against the tunnel by moving their head up and down. A third group have tall, narrow heads and squash soil to the sides by swinging their head left and right (3).

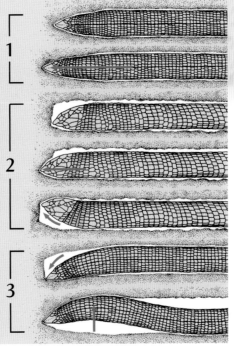

XENOSAURS

The word *xenosaur* means "strange lizard," and these reptiles certainly live up to their name. Members of this small family all have flat heads and bumpy scales. Scientists find it difficult to classify the xenosaurs.

Xenosaurs are odd-looking lizards with flattish bodies and large, knobbly scales on their backs. They range in size from 8 to 18 inches long. They have strong limbs and long, thin tails. Their bodies are covered with small scales mixed up with larger scales, forming a V-shaped pattern across the body. The ridged scales along the back and tail form a crest. These scales rise from bony plates called osteoderms, which are embedded in the skin. The flat head of the xenosaur is roughly triangular in shape. Their strong jaws contain many teeth. The short, broad tongue is slightly forked at the tip. Some species have a pair of ridges on their head, which run over the eyes to the back of the neck. Xenosaurs have fixed eyelids. Their ear openings are hidden by scales. The bodies of these reptiles are brown with pale V-shapes pointing toward the tail. Their front legs are often yellow. These subtle colors provide camouflage and help the xenosaur to blend in with the forested areas in which it lives.

Classifying Xenosaurs

Scientists have had problems classifying xenosaurs and figuring out their relationship to other groups of lizards. Their small scales suggest they are related to beaded lizards. However, the bony plates beneath their scales suggest a link with the family of slender, snakelike lizards called anguids. Xenosaurs are now placed in a group of their own.

The Chinese crocodile lizard is extremely rare in the wild. The survival of these xenosaurs depends on the success of captive breeding programs by collectors.

Fact File

XENOSAURS

Family: Xenosauridae contains six species, divided into two genera (subgroups): *Xenosaurus* (knob-scaled lizards, five species) and *Shinisaurus* (one species, the Chinese crocodile lizard)

Order: Squamata

Where do they live?: Mexico and southwestern China

Equator

Habitat: Mountain forests, usually near water

Length: 8–18 in. (20–46 cm)

Appearance: Flattish lizards with strong limbs and long tails. Larger scales form a crest running along the back and tail. Usually brown with pale, V-shaped markings pointing toward the tail

Diet: Insects and plants; Chinese crocodile lizard eats fish and tadpoles

Breeding: Females give birth to 2–10 live young

Lifespan: At least 7 years

Status: Varies from endangered to data deficient

⬤ *The Chinese crocodile lizard is often found resting on the branches above shallow ponds and streams.*

The xenosaur family contains just six species, which are divided into two subgroups. One group, commonly called the knob-scaled lizards, contains five species. These xenosaurs live in the mountains of Mexico and Guatemala in Central America. The second group contains just one species, the crocodile lizard, which lives in southwestern China. The Chinese crocodile lizard was identified in 1928, but it was not classed as a xenosaur until the 1960s. The two groups of xenosaurs are thus found on different continents, thousands of miles apart, which is extremely unusual.

So how could this widely scattered distribution of the xenosaurs have come about? Scientists explain the presence of the two groups on separate continents using the theory of tectonic drift. According to this theory, the continents sit atop huge sections of Earth's crust called tectonic plates. These plates are not fixed but slowly drift across the face of the planet, driven by churning currents in the hot, liquid rock in Earth's center. Many millions of years ago, Earth's continents were not in their present positions but linked as one huge landmass called Pangaea. Over time, the landmass gradually split apart. As the continents drifted apart, so the species that had once roamed freely across Pangaea became isolated. The discovery of xenosaur fossils in Europe, where there are no xenosaurs today, provides some support for this theory.

Breeding Habits

Xenosaurs live alone for most of the year. If two lizards meet, a fight will often break out. Males in particular will bite one another ferociously. Scientists think that these lizards breed every other year. In all species, the female carries the eggs inside her body and gives birth to living young. Litters contain between two and ten offspring. Studies of one species suggest that mothers cooperate to care for their young, which is extremely unusual. Researchers report the babies are placed in a "creche" or crib that is guarded by several females until the young are a few months old.

WAY OF LIFE

Five species of knob-scaled lizards live in forests in the mountains of Mexico and Guatemala. These creatures are usually found near water. They dwell on the ground or under stones, but some species climb into shrubs in search of food. The Chinese crocodile lizard lives near water and is a semiaquatic species. Xenosaurs are active at dusk and at night. Knob-scaled lizards feed on ants and winged termites, but the largest species also eat flowers and fruit and have been known to prey on small vertebrates. The Chinese crocodile lizard is a strong swimmer and often visits the water to catch fish, tadpoles, and other aquatic creatures.

Xenosaurs show little fear of predators or people. If an intruder appears they freeze and rely on their camouflage to hide them. If the enemy approaches, they open their mouth wide to reveal a black membrane. If this warning display fails to scare off the intruder, their powerful jaws can deliver a painful bite.

GLOSSARY

adaptation Any feature of an animal's body or behavior that makes it suited to live in a particular environment

aggression Hostile, violent, or destructive behavior

agile To be able to move quickly and easily

algae Simple, plantlike living things that grow in water or wet places and make their own food

ambush To lie in wait and make a surprise attack on a prey animal

annuli (*singular* annulus) Ringlike structures on the body of a caecilian

aquatic Living in the water

arboreal Living fully or partly in trees

Arctic The region around the North Pole

bask To lie in the Sun to warm up the body

beak The narrow, protruding jaws of a tortoise or turtle

biome A major zone of the living world, such as a desert or rain forest, and all the living things within it

burrow A tunnel or series of tunnels in the ground made by an animal in which to live

camouflage Patterns or colors that allow an animal to blend in with its surroundings to escape predators, or creep up on prey without being seen

cannibalism The eating of the flesh of an animal by another animal of the same species

captivity When an animal is held in an enclosed space, such as a farm, wildlife park, or zoo

carrion The decaying remains of dead animals

classification The process by which all living things are grouped according to similarities and differences. Classification helps scientists to study living things and to suggest how they may have evolved over time

claypan An Australian word used to describe a shallow, bowl-shaped dip in the ground where water collects after it has been raining

climate The average weather conditions in a broad region over a long period of time

clutch The group of eggs laid by a female at any one time

cocoon A tough, protective covering for an animal's body when it is developing

conservation The act of protecting the natural world and saving rare species

courtship Any behavior that occurs between males and females before mating

crustacean Water-living creatures, such as shrimp and water fleas, that form the main diet for the larval stages of many amphibians

desert A very dry region with few plants and less than ten inches of rainfall each year

dewlap A fold of loose skin that hangs from the throat of some animals

digestion The process of breaking down food into small pieces so the body can absorb it

direct development The process of development in which young amphibians hatch out of the eggs looking like adults instead of tadpoles

diurnal Active during the day

domesticated animals Animals that are farmed or tamed by people

ecosystem A habitat such as a patch of forest and all the living things found within it

embryo The early stage in the development of a living thing

estivation The sleeplike state some animals adopt in summer to avoid heat and drought

evolution The gradual process of change in species that produces new species

extinction The process by which a species dies out forever

family A group of related living things forming a classification category that ranks above a genus and below an order

fang A long, pointed tooth that may be used to deliver venom

fertilization When a female egg cell and a male sperm cell join to form a new living thing

floodplain A wide, flat area near the mouth of a river, which is often flooded when the river spills over its banks

food chain All the different feeding relationships between animals and plants

food web All the different food chains within a habitat

fungi Living things that are neither plants nor animals. Fungi cannot make their own food and feed on living things or their dead remains

gator A shortened name for an alligator, which is often used in the United States

gestation period The time an animal spends developing inside its mother's body

gill A flaplike structure in aquatic animals through which the exchange of oxygen and waste gases takes place

habitat The place in which an animal or plant lives

hatching To break free from an egg into the outside world

hatchling An animal that has just emerged from its egg

heat pit A hole containing heat-sensitive cells that are on the side of the head, or along the lips, of some groups of snakes

hibernate To spend the winter in an inactive sleeplike state to conserve energy

home range The area that an animal uses during daily activities such as foraging

hormone A chemical that is carried by the blood to other parts of the body where it causes a specific response

humus A brown or black crumbly material in the soil, which consists of the remains of plants and animals

immune The state of being resistant to poisons or disease

introduced Describes an animal or plant brought by people to an region in which it is not naturally found

invertebrate An animal without a backbone

larva The early stage in the development of an animal after hatching from an egg

leaf litter A layer of leaves and other debris that collects on the surface of the soil in woodlands

mammal An animal with fur that maintains its own temperature and feeds its young on milk

metamorphosis The change in body shape that takes place when some animals grow into their adult form

molt Shedding the skin so that it can be replaced with new skin

nocturnal Active at night

nutrient Food that gives an animal energy to grow

omnivore An animal that eats a wide range of foods, both animal and vegetable

orbital gland A gland near a vertebrate's eye that produces fluids that keep the eye moist

order A classification group ranking above family and below class

osteoderm A boney lump in a reptile's skin that provides protection against predators

placenta An organ that develops inside the mother's womb to help the embryo obtain nourishment from its mother during gestation

pod A term used to describe a group of young alligators

predator An animal that

kills and eats other animals

pregnant When a female is carrying one or more developing young inside her body

prehensile A grasping structure, such as a tail, that gives an especially strong grip

prey An animal that is caught and eaten by another animal

rain forest A habitat that is hot and wet all year round and is dominated by tall trees that form an overhead canopy

scale A thin, platelike structure that forms part of the surface covering of various vertebrates, such as reptiles and fishes

scrubland A dry habitat that is dominated by plants such as low-growing shrubs

shrubland A biome that contains plants such as shrubs and short trees

skull The boney framework that encases and protects a vertebrate's brain

species A scientific term that means a type of living thing that can breed with others of its own kind to produce offspring that can also interbreed successfully

suffocation Killing an animal by stopping it breathing

tadpole The earliest stage of development of an amphibian

temperate zones Two broad regions of the Earth between the Tropic of Cancer and the Arctic Circle in the north and the Tropic of Capricorn and the

Antarctic Circle in the south

tentacles Slender, flexible organs on an animal's head, which are for feeling, exploring or grasping

terrestrial Living wholly or partly on the ground

territory A feeding or breeding area occupied by one animal or a group of animals of the same species

transparent Something that is seethrough

tropical grassland Hot grassland, with wet and dry seasons, which occurs both north and south of the equator

venom A chemical produce by some animals that can paralyze or kill prey or predators

vertebrate An animal with a backbone. All amphibians and reptiles are vertebrates

warning color The bright color on an animal's body that warns it is poisonous or tastes bad and should be left alone

webbed feet Having skin stretched between the toes, which helps the animal to swim

wetland A habitat with a lot of water on the surface, ranging from marshes, swamps, and flooded forests to rivers, streams, and lakes

yolk sac A large sac containing stored nutrients, which is used to feed the embryos of reptiles and amphibians

FURTHER RESOURCES

BOOKS

Beltz, Ellin. *Frogs: Inside Their Remarkable World.* Firefly, 2005.

Davies, Valerie. *Incredible Reptiles (Wild Life!).* School Specialty Publishing, 2007.

Harrison, Paul. *Reptiles (Up Close).* PowerKids Press, 2007.

Harrison, Paul. *Snakes (Up Close).* PowerKids Press, 2007.

Huggins-Copper, Lynn. *Ravenous Reptiles (Killer Nature!).* Smart Apple Media, 2006.

Huggins-Copper, Lynn. *Revolting Reptiles and Awful Amphibians (Qeb Awesome Animals).* Qeb Pub, 2008.

Huggins-Copper, Lynn. *Slithering Snakes (Killer Nature!).* Smart Apple Media, 2006.

Johnson, Sylvia A. *Cobras (Nature Watch).* Lerner Publications, 2007.

Mattison, Chris, Val Davies, and David Alderton. *Reptiles and Amphibians (Facts at Your Fingertips).* Brown Bear Books, 2007.

Miller, Ruth. *Reptiles (Animal Kingdom).* Raintree, 2005.

Otfinoski, S. *Alligators (Animals Animals).* Benchmark Books, 2008.

Parket, Janice. *Reptiles (Life Science).* Weigl Publishers, 2007.

Rebman, Renee. *Turtles and Tortoises.* Benchmark Books, 2007.

Singer, Marilyn. *Venom.* Darby Creek Publishing, 2007.

Sneddon, Robert. *Amphibians (Living Things).* Smart Apple Media, 2007.

Sneddon, Robert. *Reptiles (Living Things).* Smart Apple Media, 2007.

Solway, Andrew. *Deadly Reptiles (Wild Predators).* Heinemann, 2005.

Somerville, Louisa. *Snakes (World of Animals).* Brown Bear Reference, 2008.

Stone, Lynne M. *Box Turtles (Nature Watch).* Lerner Publications, 2007.

Taylor, Barbara. *Nature Watch: Snakes.* Lorenz Books, 2008.

Townsend, John. *Incredible Reptiles.* Raintree, 2005.

Williams, Brian. *Amazing Reptiles and Amphibians (Amazing Life Cycles).* Gareth Stevens Publishing, 2007.

Wilsdon, C. *Snakes (Amazing Animals).* Gareth Stevens Publishing, 2008.

INTERNET RESOURCES

All About Reptiles
Detailed account of reptiles and amphibians, with some fantastic links to more information.
www.livescience.com/reptiles

Amphibians and Reptiles of Europe
Web site with lots of image and information about little-known amphibians and reptiles.
www.herp.it

Amphibians and Reptiles of North Carolina
A comprehensive study of North Carolina's cold-blooded fauna.
www.herpsofnc.org

AmphibiaWeb
Detailed Web site that lets you search amphibians by family and location.
www.amphibiaweb.org

California Reptiles and Amphibians
A fascinating study of all the reptiles and amphibians in California in the United States.
www.californiaherps.com

Enchanted Learning
Check out everything to do with reptiles.
www.enchantedlearning.com/subjects/reptiles/printouts.shtml

Exploratorium: Frogs
Another great exhibit from the Exploratorium includes cool information and activities. Check out the frog tracker for great frog sounds.
www.exploratorium.edu/frogs

Guide to Reptiles, Amphibians, and Herps
Not-for-profit organization set up to help save animals and plants.
www.reptilesweb.com

Herper charity website
Information about reptiles and amphibians and how to look after them.
www.herper.com

Iowa and Minnesota
Field guides to the reptiles and amphibians of the two states.
www.herpnet.net

IUCN Red List of Threatened Species
Worldwide assessment of the conservation status of species of living organisms.
www.iucnredlist.org

Reptile and Amphibian Resources for Kids
Full of Web sites to visit to find out more about amphibians and reptiles.
http://research.calacademy.org/research/library/biodiv/biblio/zrepamph.htm

Society for the Study of Amphibians and Reptiles
Charity to promote the conservation and education of amphibians and reptiles worldwide.
www.ssarherps.org

World Wildlife Fund
Find out more about wildlife conservation
www.worldwildlife.org

Yahooligans!
An introduction to amphibians and reptiles. Click on the links to find out more information.
www.kids.yahoo.com/animals

SET INDEX